NOT BY
BREAD ALONE

Proverbs of the Bible

Wolfgang Mieder

Woodcuts by Mary Azarian

*For Robyn,
with good wishes
Wolfy
September 7, 2003*

The New England Press
Shelburne, Vermont

For additional copies of this book or for a catalog
of our other titles, please write:

The New England Press
P.O. Box 575
Shelburne, VT 05482

Contents

Introduction

Of all books ever written, the Bible is without doubt the most widely known and read, having been translated into just about every language throughout the world. For centuries in Europe and America, it was *the* book in every household. During religious services worshippers would hear its message read to them, or they would recite passages in unison. The Bible was studied at home and in school, and many verses were memorized and quoted orally as the occasion arose. Knowledge of the religious and practical wisdom of the Bible was common in all strata of society. People knew their Bible, and they quoted it frequently in oral and written communication. To this day, the Bible must be considered part of the western cultural heritage and literacy since it forms the basis for our moral and ethical codes of behavior. It clearly remains the gospel for believers, although references to biblical passages and motifs abound in secular literature, mass media, and everyday communication.

A book of such significance and international distribution greatly influenced the many languages into which it was rendered. Its early Hebrew, Greek, and Latin texts show that the prophets and evangelists used a style that was based largely on folk language, assuring from the beginning clear and meaningful communication with all followers. To be sure, numerous psalms and passages in all books of the Bible are expressed in poetic and even mystical language, but many individual verses also include folk wisdom in the form of common proverbs. Much of the Bible derives from wisdom literature, an ancient tradition that has been traced back to Aramaic, Assyrian, Egyptian, Phoenician, and even Sumerian sources. This international body of norms, rules, and values for proper human behavior also influenced the Jewish, Greek, and Roman cultures, and much of it remains valid and current to this day.

The Old Testament and the Apocrypha especially contain much of this wisdom literature in the form of riddles, fables, and proverbs. The books of Job, Proverbs, and Ecclesiastes are in fact referred to as the wisdom books by biblical scholars. To these may be added the books of Ecclesiasticus and The Wisdom of Solomon from the Apocrypha. Their authors espoused the belief that wisdom can and must be taught, and their texts are filled with short statements of authoritative instruction, behavioral advice, social and ethical imperatives, and other types of paradigmatic truths. Proverbs by their nature are the most concise expressions of worldly wisdom, and they existed in biblical times both in oral communication and in early collections. As formulaic and generally known statements, they were ready to be incorporated into the Bible as didactic and ethical precepts.

The evangelists of the New Testament had a respectful attitude toward this ancient wisdom literature. They often cited proverbs from the Old Testament, which formed a bridge between the old Jewish folk wisdom and the proverbial wisdom that later emerged in the vernacular languages. The four Synoptic Gospels especially include much practical wisdom in proverbial form. Most of these proverbs repeat observations concerning common human experiences from the Old Testament. They advise people on how to deal with everyday life and its problems. These writers hoped to jolt the believers into new and better judgments concerning their lives by couching many of the texts in paradoxical or antithetical statements. Jesus' use of such proverbs as "It is easier for a camel to go through the eye of a needle, than for a rich man to enter into the kingdom of God" (Matt. 19:24; Mark 10:25) and "The first shall be last, and the last shall be first" (Matt. 19:30, 20:16; Mark 10:31; Luke 13:30) particularly indicate this attempt at existential reorientation. Jesus' instructional speech is certainly based on the oral tradition of proverbs, and his gift of putting proverbial folk language to practical use helped spread his new gospel.

A considerable amount of scholarship exists on the origins of some of the biblical proverbs. Identifying origins is particularly difficult since the general currency of these proverbs at the time the Bible was written is very difficult if not impossible to establish. It would be a great mistake to conclude that the Book of Proverbs consists entirely of folk proverbs—nothing could be further from the truth. But the Book of Proverbs certainly contains the most proverbs of any book in the Bible, and many continue their existence in word-for-word translations in many languages. Such internationally disseminated proverbs include, among numerous others, "Pride goes before a fall" (Prov. 16:18), "Hatred stirs up strife" (Prov. 10:12), and "Answer a fool according to his folly" (Prov. 26:4–5).

Some biblical proverbs have gained particularly widespread popularity in the English language. From the Old Testament we might cite "In the sweat of your brows shall you eat bread" (Gen. 3:19), "The Lord gives, and the Lord takes away" (Job 1:21), "The price of a virtuous woman is far above rubies" (Prov. 31:10), "There is nothing new under the sun" (Eccles. 1:9), and "A leopard cannot change his spots" (Jer. 13:23). Also very popular is the proverb "Health is better than wealth" (Ecclus. 30:15) from the Apocrypha. To the truly "classical" New Testament proverbs belong "A prophet is not without honor save in his own country" (Matt. 13:57; Mark 6:4; Luke 4:24; John 4:44), "The spirit is willing, but the flesh is weak" (Matt. 26:41; Mark 14:38), "Let the one without sin cast the first stone"

(John 8:7), "It is better to give than to receive" (Acts 20:35), and "The love of money is the root of all evil" (1 Tim. 6:10). Many proverbs reappear numerous times throughout the Bible, and it should not surprise us that these proverbs continue to be frequently used today, such as "An eye for an eye, and a tooth for a tooth" (Exod. 21:24; Lev. 24:20; Deut. 19:21; Matt. 5:39), "Beat your swords into plowshares and your spears into pruning hooks" (Isa. 2:4; Joel 3:10; Mic. 4:3), "Eat, drink and be merry" (Eccles. 8:15; Luke 12:19), and *the* biblical proverb, "Man cannot live by bread alone" (Deut. 8:3; Matt. 4:4; Luke 4:4).

The prophets and evangelists delighted in citing two similar proverbs together, to assure that their message would not be lost. Mindful that "two are better than one" (Eccles. 4:9), we find such proverb pairs as "A dog returns to his vomit" and "A fool returns to his folly" (Prov. 26:11); "No man can serve two masters" and "You cannot serve God and Mammon" (Matt. 6:24); and "Beware of false prophets" and "Beware of a wolf in sheep's clothing" (Matt. 7:15). An educational string of proverbs concerns time: "There is a time for everything," "There is a time to be born, and a time to die," "There is a time to weep, and a time to laugh," "There is a time to speak, and a time to be silent," and "There is a time to love, and a time to hate" (Eccles. 3:1-2, 4, 7-8).

Many of the proverbs in this collection are identical to texts of the King James Bible or were varied only slightly by folk speech. But some Anglo-American proverbs were coined as allusions to certain biblical passages. These are not direct quotes from the Bible but are merely of biblical origin. Thus, while the Bible states "He that spareth his rod hateth his son: but he that loveth him chasteneth him betimes" (Prov. 13:24), the English folk proverb instructs more succinctly, "Spare the rod and spoil the child." It has existed in this precise form since the seventeenth century. The biblical proverb "It is not good to eat much honey" (Prov. 25:27) has been cited since the sixteenth century as the folk proverb "Too much honey cloys the stomach." Other rephrasings and allusions to biblical passages include the current "The devil can cite Scripture for his purpose" (Matt. 4:6), "Birds of a feather flock together" (Ecclus. 27:9), "Man proposes, God disposes" (Prov. 16:9), and even the proverbial weather forecast "Red sky at night, is a shepherd's delight, / red sky in the morning, is a shepherd's warning" (Matt. 16:2–3). Biblical texts are clearly not sacrosanct when it comes to citing them as folk proverbs; more often than not, speakers are not even aware that they are using a proverb partly derived from the Bible.

Not all proverbs original to the Bible remained proverbial in the languages and cultures into which they were translated. Some translators lacked the skill to find the aesthetic form and structure necessary for a statement to become a proverb. Nevertheless, the languages of most cultures for which the Bible is the major spiritual book contain between three hundred and five hundred proverbs that stem from the Bible. In English, at least 425 distinct proverbs have their origin in the Bible. Of these, 212 are from the Old Testament, thirty-one are from the Apocrypha, and 182 are from the New Testament. Not surprisingly, one hundred of the English proverbs go back to the Book of Proverbs, while forty are from Ecclesiastes, eleven from Psalms, and ten each from Job and Isaiah. The remaining forty-two proverbs are distributed throughout other books of the Old Testament. From the Apocrypha, twenty-five proverbs of Ecclesiasticus are still current in our culture. The statistics for the New Testament are a bit more difficult to pinpoint, due primarily to the repetitiveness of the Synoptic Gospels. Matthew, the primary gospel, contains seventy-six proverbs, of which many are cited again in other books of the New Testament. John contains fourteen additional proverbs, Luke cites ten distinct texts, and Mark adds one further text to those found in Matthew. A considerable level of proverbiality is also reached by 1 Corinthians (eighteen texts), Romans (seventeen), and James (ten). But the 425 total proverbs represent truly distinct texts within the entire Bible. Were one to include all the repetitions, this number would easily be increased by at least threefold.

In this book, we have divided the 425 proverbs into nineteen thematic chapters with an average twenty-two texts each. The titles of these chapters clearly indicate that the biblical proverbs current in our culture are not necessarily deeply religious or sacred. Even those proverbs referring to God and faith are practical bits of wisdom based on everyday human experience and observation. The wisdom is expressed in colloquial metaphors that have little to do with religious concerns. In fact, some of them are downright questionable, like the chauvinistic "A woman is the weaker vessel" (1 Pet. 3:7). This and other proverbs like it should not be used in a society in which the emancipation and equality of women are major issues.

Proverbs are not universal truths, not even the proverbs from the Bible. Their wisdom or apparent truth always depends on a social context, where they usually express the only-too-human problems and concerns of good and evil, parents and children, love and friendship, wisdom and folly, wealth and poverty, time and chance, deception and appearance, work and laziness, and advice and prudence. Even without reading or consciously quoting from the Bible, these "proverbs among all people" (see 1 Kings 9:7) help us all communicate with each other in everyday encounters, basing our moral judgments and social behavior on an ethical and religious value system that has withstood the test of time.

Abbreviations

(only those books of the Bible that contain proverbs are listed; cross-references to parallel biblical citations of individual proverbs are kept to a minimum)

Old Testament:

Gen.	Genesis
Exod.	Exodus
Lev.	Leviticus
Deut.	Deuteronomy
Judg.	Judges
1 Sam.	1 Samuel
1 Kings	1 Kings
1 Chron.	1 Chronicles
2 Chron.	2 Chronicles
Job	Job
Ps.	Psalms
Prov.	Proverbs
Eccles.	Ecclesiastes
Song of Sol.	Song of Solomon
Isa.	Isaiah
Jer.	Jeremiah
Lam.	Lamentations
Ezek.	Ezekiel
Dan.	Daniel
Hos.	Hosea
Joel	Joel
Amos	Amos
Mic.	Micah
Hab.	Habakkuk
Zech.	Zechariah

Apocrypha:

1 Esd.	1 Esdras
2 Esd.	2 Esdras
Wisd. of Sol.	The Wisdom of Solomon
Ecclus.	Ecclesiasticus
2 Macc.	2 Maccabees

New Testament:

Matt.	Matthew
Mark	Mark
Luke	Luke
John	John
Acts	Acts of the Apostles
Rom.	Romans
1 Cor.	1 Corinthians
2 Cor.	2 Corinthians
Gal.	Galatians
Eph.	Ephesians
1 Thess.	1 Thessalonians
2 Thess.	2 Thessalonians
1 Tim.	1 Timothy
2 Tim.	2 Timothy
Titus	Titus
Heb.	Hebrews
James	James
1 Pet.	1 Peter
2 Pet.	2 Peter
1 John	1 John
Rev.	Revelation

GOOD
— AND —
EVIL

Evil communications corrupt
good manners.
(1 Cor. 15:33)

That which is crooked cannot be
made straight.
(Eccles. 1:15)

Overcome evil with good.
(Rom. 12:21)

Hell and destruction are never full.
(Prov. 27:20)

Wickedness proceeds from the wicked.
(1 Sam. 24:13)

He who mocks another shall be mocked.
(Job 13:9)

Blessed are the pure at heart.
(Matt. 5:8)

Let not the sun go down upon
your wrath.
(Eph. 4:26)

The heart knows its own bitterness.
(Prov. 14:10)

Never be weary of well-doing.
(Gal. 6:9; 2 Thess. 3:19)

Abhor what is evil and cleave to
what is good.
(Rom. 12:9)

Do good for evil.
(1 Thess. 5:15)

Resist the devil, and he will
flee from you.
(James 4:7)

Sufficient unto the day is
the evil thereof.
(Matt. 6:34)

The wicked flee when no man pursues.
(Prov. 28:1)

To the pure all things are pure.
(Titus 1:15)

There is no man who doesn't sin.
(1 Kings 8:46)

Never do evil that good may come of it.
(Rom. 3:8)

Like tree, like fruit.
(Matt. 7:18; Luke 6:43)

The way of transgressors is hard.
(Prov. 13:15)

Don't render evil for good.
(1 Sam. 25:21)

He that does ill, hates the light.
(John 3:20)

A stubborn heart shall fare evil at last.
(Ecclus. 3:26)

You can see a mote in another's eye but
cannot see a beam in your own.
(Matt. 7:3; Luke 6:41)

PROPHECY
AND
PREDICTION

A prophet is not without honor save in
his own country.
(Matt. 13:57; Mark 6:4; Luke 4:24; John 4:44)

Watch for the handwriting on the wall.
(Dan. 5:5)

A good name endures forever.
(Ecclus. 41:13)

Let him that thinks he stands take
heed lest he fall.
(1 Cor. 10:12)

Pride goes before a fall.
(Prov. 16:18)

A man that flatters his neighbor
spreads a net for his feet.
(Prov. 29:5)

The last error shall be worse
than the first.
(Matt. 27:64)

The wolf shall dwell with the lamb,
and the leopard shall lie down
with the kid.
(Isa. 11:6)

Unto everyone that has shall be given,
but from him that has not
shall be taken away.
(Matt. 13:12, 25:29; Mark 4:25; Luke 8:18, 19:26)

To whom much is given much shall
be required.
(Luke 12:48)

By their fruits you shall know them.
(Matt. 7:16, 7:20)

Give, and it shall be given unto you.
(Luke 6:38)

The kingdom of heaven is like to a
grain of mustard seed.
(Matt. 13:31)

It's a book sealed with seven seals.
(Rev. 5:1)

The meek shall inherit the earth.
(Ps. 37:11; Matt. 5:5)

He that touches pitch shall be defiled.
(Ecclus. 13:1)

Charity never fails.
(1 Cor. 13:8)

Blessed are the peacemakers.
(Matt. 5:9)

Constant dropping will wear the stone.
(Job 14:19)

Charity covers a multitude of sins.
(1 Pet. 4:8)

The merciful shall obtain mercy.
(Matt. 5:7)

As a tree falls, so shall it lie.
(Eccles. 11:3)

The axe is laid unto the root
of the trees.
(Matt. 3:10)

Red sky at night,
is a shepherd's delight,
red sky in the morning,
is a shepherd's warning.
(Matt. 16:2–3)

Don't seek the living among the dead.
(Luke 24:5)

When pride comes, shame also comes.
(Prov. 11:2)

Out of the mouths of babes and
sucklings you have perfect praise.
(Matt 21:16)

The curse that is causeless
shall not come.
(Prov. 26:2)

The wages of sin is death.
(Rom. 6:23)

He that despises small things shall
fall little by little.
(Ecclus. 19:1)

Where the carcass is, there will the
eagles be gathered together.
(Matt. 24:28; Luke 17:37)

Is Saul also among the prophets?
(1 Sam. 10:11–12)

Boast not of tomorrow, for you know
not what a day may bring forth.
(Prov. 27:1)

The truth shall make you free.
(John 8:32)

PARENTS
— AND —
CHILDREN

Spare the rod and spoil the child.
(Prov. 13:24)

Like mother, like daughter.
(Ezek. 16:44)

A foolish son is the calamity
of his father.
(Prov. 19:13)

In malice be children, but in
understanding be men.
(1 Cor. 14:20)

Even a child is known by his doings.
(Prov. 20:11)

Woe to the kingdom whose king
is a child.
(Eccles. 10:16)

The branch cannot bear fruit
by itself.
(John 15:4)

A poor and wise child is better than
an old and foolish king.
(Eccles. 4:13)

A wise son makes a glad father.
(Prov. 10:1)

Miss not the discourse of the elders.
(Ecclus. 8:9)

The fathers have eaten sour grapes
and the children's teeth are
set on edge.
(Jer. 31:29; Ezek. 18:2)

LOVE
AND
FRIENDSHIP

Many waters cannot quench love nor
can floods drown it.
(Song of Sol. 8:7)

Love your enemies.
(Matt. 5:44; Luke 6:27)

Perfect love casts out fear.
(1 John 4:18)

Better is a neighbor that is near
than a brother far off.
(Prov. 27:10)

Open rebuke is better than secret love.
(Prov. 27:5)

There is a time to love, and a
time to hate.
(Eccles. 3:8)

Two cannot walk together except
they be agreed.
(Amos 3:3)

A faithful friend is the medicine of life.
(Ecclus. 6:16)

Am I my brother's keeper?
(Gen. 4:9)

Love covers all sins.
(Prov. 10:12)

A new friend is as new wine;
when it is old, you shall drink it
with pleasure.
(Ecclus. 9:10)

Live peaceably with all men.
(Rom. 12:18)

He that would have friends must show
himself friendly.
(Prov. 18:24)

A threefold cord is not quickly broken.
(Eccles. 4:12)

A righteous man regards the life
of his animal.
(Prov. 12:10)

Love your neighbor as yourself.
(Lev. 19:18, Matt. 19:19; Mark 12:31; Rom. 13:9;
Gal. 5:14; James 2:8)

There is a friend that sticks closer
than a brother.
(Prov. 18:24)

Love is strong as death.
(Song of Sol. 8:6)

Better a dinner of herbs where love is,
than a stalled ox where hate is.
(Prov. 15:17)

SPEAKING
— AND —
HEARING

The tongue can break a bone though
itself has none.
(Prov. 25:15)

Out of the abundance of the heart
the mouth speaks.
(Matt. 12:34; Luke 6:45)

There is a time to speak, and a time
to be silent.
(Eccles. 3:7)

Be swift to hear, slow to speak,
and slow to wrath.
(James 1:19)

He that has knowledge spares his words.
(Prov. 17:27)

Answering before hearing is folly.
(Prov. 18:13)

It is foolish to make a long prologue
and to be short in the story itself.
(2 Macc. 2:32)

A word spoken in due season is good.
(Prov. 15:23)

He that has ears to hear, let him hear.
(Matt. 11:15, 13:9; Mark 4:9; Rev. 2:7)

A whisperer separates friends.
(Prov. 16:28)

Nobody can tame the tongue.
(James 3:8)

A soft answer turns away wrath.
(Prov. 15:1)

Words are but wind.
(Job 6:26)

The discourse of fools is irksome.
(Ecclus. 27:13)

The eye is not satisfied with seeing,
nor the ear filled with hearing.
(Eccles. 1:8)

Out of the same mouth proceed
blessing and cursing.
(James 3:10)

He that guards his mouth keeps his
life, but he that opens wide his lips
shall have destruction.
(Prov. 13:3)

The stroke of the whip makes marks
in the flesh, but the stroke of the
tongue breaks bones.
(Ecclus. 28:17)

A word fitly spoken is like apples of
gold in pictures of silver.
(Prov. 25:11)

FAITH
— AND —
SPIRIT

Man cannot live by bread alone.
(Deut. 8:3; Matt. 4:4; Luke 4:4)

Of faith, hope and charity the
greatest is charity.
(1 Cor. 13:13)

Ask, and it shall be given you.
(Matt. 7:7; John 16:24)

Faith without works is dead.
(James 2:20)

He that endures to the end
shall be saved.
(Matt. 10:22; Mark 13:13)

Hope deferred makes the heart sick.
(Prov. 13:12)

Fight the good fight of faith.
(1 Tim. 6:12)

The letter kills, but the spirit gives life.
(2 Cor. 3:6)

The just shall live by faith.
(Rom. 1:17; Heb. 10:38)

Cast your bread upon the waters,
for you shall find it after many days.
(Eccles. 11:1)

Faith will move mountains.
(Matt. 17:20)

We walk by faith, not by sight.
(2 Cor. 5:7)

Hope makes not ashamed.
(Rom. 5:5)

Be not faithless, but believing.
(John 20:27)

Seek, and you shall find.
(Matt. 7:7; Luke 11:9)

Absent in body, but present in spirit.
(1 Cor. 5:3)

The spirit is willing, but the
flesh is weak.
(Matt. 26:41; Mark 14:38)

WISDOM
── AND ──
FOLLY

Answer a fool according to his folly.
(Prov. 26:4–5)

Wisdom is better than strength.
(Eccles. 9:16)

Fools will be meddling.
(Prov. 20:3)

Zeal without knowledge is the
sister of folly.
(Rom. 10:2)

Knowledge puffs up,
but charity edifies.
(1 Cor. 8:1)

A fool's mouth is his destruction.
(Prov. 18:7)

Fools are wise as long as they are silent.
(Prov. 17:28)

The poor man's wisdom is despised.
(Eccles. 9:16)

A reproof enters more into a wise man
than a hundred stripes into a fool.
(Prov. 17:10)

Knowledge is power.
(Prov. 24:5)

Too much learning makes men mad.
(Acts 26:24)

Wisdom is better than gold.
(Prov. 16:16)

He that increases knowledge
increases sorrow.
(Eccles. 1:18)

A fool believes everything.
(Prov. 14:15)

Great men are not always wise.
(Job 32:9)

The way of a fool is right in
his own eyes.
(Prov. 12:15)

A man that hides his foolishness is
better than a man that hides
his wisdom.
(Ecclus. 41:15)

Consider the ways of the ant
and be wise.
(Prov. 6:6)

Wisdom gives life to them that have it.
(Eccles. 7:12)

Walk with the wise men and you
shall be wise.
(Prov. 13:20)

Wisdom is the greatest thing.
(Prov. 4:7)

Be wise as serpents and harmless
as doves.
(Matt. 10:16)

He that trusts in his own heart
is a fool.
(Prov. 28:26)

Wisdom excels folly as light
excels darkness.
(Eccles. 2:13)

Even if you bray a fool in a mortar,
you cannot make him leave his folly.
(Prov. 27:22)

Wisdom is justified by her children.
(Matt. 11:19; Luke 7:35)

There is more hope of a fool than of
him that is wise in his own eyes.
(Prov. 26:12)

The words of the wise are as goads.
(Eccles. 12:11)

A fool returns to his folly.
(Prov. 26:11)

In much wisdom is much grief.
(Eccles. 1:18)

A fool utters all his mind.
(Prov. 29:11)

Suffer fools gladly.
(2 Cor. 11:19)

A whip for the horse, a bridle
for the ass, and a rod for the
back of fools.
(Prov. 26:3)

The price of wisdom is above rubies.
(Job 28:18; Prov. 8:11)

LAW
AND
JUDGMENT

An eye for an eye, and a tooth
for a tooth.
(Exod. 21:24; Lev. 24:20; Deut. 19:21; Matt. 5:38)

Do unto others as you would they
should do unto you.
(Matt. 7:12; Luke 6:31)

The tree is known by its fruit.
(Matt. 12:33; Luke 6:44)

Let all things be done in order.
(1 Cor. 14:40)

Precept must be upon precept.
(Isa. 28:10)

They that sow the wind shall reap
the whirlwind.
(Hos. 8:7)

The first shall be last, and the last
shall be first.
(Matt. 19:30, 20:16; Mark 10:31; Luke 13:30)

Let the one without sin cast
the first stone.
(John 8:7)

Truth is mighty and will prevail.
(1 Esd. 4:41)

Do as I say, not as I do.
(Matt. 23:3)

Where no law is there is no transgression.
(Rom. 4:15)

All rivers run into the sea.
(Eccles. 1:7)

Better one die than all.
(John 11:50)

In the mouth of two or three
witnesses every word may be established.
(Matt. 18:16; 2 Cor. 13:1)

To obey is better than to sacrifice.
(1 Sam. 15:22)

Judge nothing before the time.
(1 Cor. 4:5)

Let your yea be yea,
and your nay, nay.
(James 5:12)

Many are called, but few are chosen.
(Matt. 20:16, 22:14)

Better is a little with righteousness
than great revenues with injustice.
(Prov. 16:8)

With what measure you measure it shall
be measured unto you.
(Matt. 7:2; Mark 4:24; Luke 6:38)

The law is good if you use it lawfully.
(1 Tim. 1:8)

Judge not, that you be not judged.
(Matt. 7:1; Luke 6:37)

Wherein you judge another you
condemn yourself.
(Rom. 2:1)

Skin for skin.
(Job 2:4)

He that is not with me is against me.
(Matt. 12:30; Luke 11:23)

The law is open.
(Acts 19:38)

Render unto Caesar the things
which are Caesar's.
(Matt. 22:21; Mark 12:17; Luke 20:25)

JOY
AND
CONTENTMENT

Eat, drink, and be merry.
(Eccles. 8:15; Luke 12:19)

Good wine makes a merry heart.
(Ps. 104:15)

Let not your heart be troubled.
(John 14:1)

A merry heart makes a
cheerful countenance.
(Prov. 15:13)

Who sows in tears shall reap in joy.
(Ps. 126:5)

It is better to enjoy a little
with quietness than to possess much
with trouble.
(Eccles. 4:6)

Stolen waters are sweet.
(Prov. 9:17)

Call no man happy before his death.
(Ecclus. 11:28)

A merry heart does good like medicine.
(Prov. 17:22)

Rejoice with them that rejoice,
and weep with them that weep.
(Rom. 12:15)

To the hungry soul every bitter
thing is sweet.
(Prov. 27:7)

Wine makes merry.
(Eccles. 10:19)

A good conscience is a continual feast.
(Prov. 15:15)

Let us eat and drink, for tomorrow
we shall die.
(Isa. 22:13; 1 Cor. 15:32)

VANITY
AND
TRANSIENCE

Vanity of vanities; all is vanity.
(Eccles. 1:2, 1:14, 12:8)

You can't call again the day that is past.
(2 Esd. 4:5)

The fashion of this world passes away.
(1 Cor. 7:31)

Life is a span.
(Ps. 39:5)

All are of the same dust.
(Eccles. 3:20)

Flesh is frail.
(Matt. 26:41; Mark 14:38)

Every man at his best state is vanity.
(Ps. 39:5)

Dust to dust.
(Gen. 3:19)

All flesh is grass.
(Isa. 40:6; 1 Pet. 1:24)

We brought nothing into the world,
and we can carry nothing out.
(1 Tim. 6:7)

All men must die.
(Ps. 89:48)

One generation passes away,
and another generation comes.
(Eccles. 1:4)

Our days on the earth are as a shadow.
(1 Chron. 29:15; Job 8:9)

Remember the end.
(Lam. 1:9; Ecclus. 7:36, 28:6, 38:20)

There is a time to be born,
and a time to die.
(Eccles. 3:2)

WEALTH
— AND —
POVERTY

The love of money is the root of all evil.
(1 Tim. 6:10)

Wealth makes many friends.
(Prov. 19:4)

There are no riches above a sound body.
(Ecclus. 30:16)

He that gives to the poor shall not lack.
(Prov. 28:27)

Give alms of what you have.
(Luke 11:41)

It is better to give than to receive.
(Acts 20:35)

The destruction of the poor
is their poverty.
(Prov. 10:15)

The rich has many friends.
(Prov. 14:20)

Don't become a beggar by banqueting
upon borrowing.
(Ecclus. 18:33)

He that blames would buy.
(Prov. 20:14)

Pay what you owe.
(Matt. 18:28)

He that trusts in his riches shall fall.
(Prov. 11:28)

Where the treasure is, the heart will be.
(Matt. 6:21; Luke 12:34)

A man's gift makes room for him.
(Prov. 18:16)

Money answers all things.
(Eccles. 10:19)

The borrower is servant to the lender.
(Prov. 22:7)

It is better to die than to beg.
(Ecclus. 40:28)

He that makes haste to be rich shall
not be innocent.
(Prov. 28:20)

Owe no man anything.
(Rom. 13:8)

He that will be a surety for another
shall pay.
(Prov. 11:15)

Health is better than wealth.
(Ecclus. 30:15)

Treasures of wickedness
profit nothing.
(Prov. 10:2)

It is easier for a camel to go
through the eye of a needle, than for
a rich man to enter into the
kingdom of God.
(Matt. 19:24; Mark 10:25)

The poor you will always have
with you.
(Matt. 26:11; Mark 14:7; John 12:8)

A good name is better than
great riches.
(Prov. 22:1)

If riches increase, do not set your
heart upon them.
(Ps. 62:10)

That which is given to the poor is
lent to God.
(Prov. 19:17)

Riches have wings.
(Prov. 23:5)

You cannot serve God and Mammon.
(Matt. 6:24; Luke 16:13)

HATE
— AND —
STRIFE

He who lives by the sword dies
by the sword.
(Matt. 26:52)

A brother offended is harder to be
won than a strong city.
(Prov. 18:19)

Envy and wrath shorten the life.
(Ecclus. 30:24)

Oppression makes the wise man mad.
(Eccles. 7:7)

Turn the other cheek.
(Matt. 5:39; Luke 6:29)

Every kingdom divided against
itself soon falls.
(Matt. 12:25; Mark 3:25; Luke 11:17)

He that troubles his own house shall
inherit the wind.
(Prov. 11:29)

We roar like bears, and mourn
like doves.
(Isa. 59:11)

He that is slow to anger is better
than the mighty.
(Prov. 16:32)

The ear of jealousy hears all things.
(Wisd. of Sol. 1:10)

Don't remove the neighbor's landmark.
(Deut. 27:17; Prov. 22:28, 23:10)

The sting is in the tail.
(Rev. 9:10)

Better a dry morsel and quietness
with it, than a house full of
feasting with strife.
(Prov. 17:1)

Blood will have blood.
(Gen. 9:6)

The wringing of the nose brings
forth blood.
(Prov. 30:33)

There's nothing worse than an enemy
of one's own household.
(Matt. 10:36)

Jealousy is cruel as the grave.
(Song of Sol. 8:6)

Hatred stirs up strife.
(Prov. 10:12)

A house divided against itself
shall not stand.
(Matt. 12:25; Mark 3:25; Luke 11:17)

Beat your swords into plowshares and
your spears into pruning hooks.
(Isa. 2:4; Joel 3:10; Mic. 4:3)

ACTIONS
AND
CONSEQUENCES

One sows and another reaps.
(John 4:37)

Let another man praise you and not
your own mouth.
(Prov. 27:2)

Give credit where credit is due.
(Rom. 13:7)

Don't strain at a gnat and
swallow a camel.
(Matt. 23:24)

Much study is weariness of the flesh.
(Eccles. 12:12)

Put not your trust in princes.
(Ps. 146:3)

The dog to his vomit and the sow
to her mire.
(2 Pet. 2:22)

The devil can cite Scripture
for his purpose.
(Matt. 4:6)

The truth endures.
(1 Esd. 4:38)

Physician, heal thyself.
(Luke 4:23)

May we not do what we like
with our own?
(Matt. 20:15)

As the man is, so is his strength.
(Judg. 8:21)

Remember Lot's wife.
(Luke 17:32)

Righteousness exalts a nation,
but sin is a reproach to any people.
(Prov. 14:34)

Let the dead bury the dead.
(Matt. 8:22; Luke 9:60)

Better eye out than always ache.
(Matt. 18:9)

There are wheels within wheels.
(Ezek. 1:16)

Give everyone his due.
(Rom. 13:7)

Charity grows cold.
(Matt. 24:12)

He that runs may read.
(Hab. 2:2)

The left hand doesn't know what the
right hand is doing.
(Matt. 6:3)

Iron whets iron.
(Prov. 27:17)

Dead flies corrupt the most
precious ointments.
(Eccles. 10:1)

They that be whole need not a
physician, but they that are sick.
(Matt. 9:12; Mark 2:17; Luke 5:31)

Forgive them, for they know not
what they do.
(Luke 23:34)

TIME
AND
CHANCE

There is a time for everything.
(Eccles. 3:1)

The sun shines upon all alike.
(Matt. 5:45)

In vain the net is spread in the sight
of the bird.
(Prov. 1:17)

Wide is the gate and broad is the way
that leads to destruction.
(Matt. 7:13)

The hour has not yet come.
(John 2:4)

As your days are, so shall your
strength be.
(Deut. 33:25)

Many run in a race but one
receives the prize.
(1 Cor. 9:24)

There is nothing new under the sun.
(Eccles. 1:9)

Be instant in season and out of season.
(2 Tim. 4:2)

You know not what tomorrow shall be.
(James 4:14)

There is a time to weep, and a
time to laugh.
(Eccles. 3:4)

The wind blows where it lists.
(John 3:8)

The race is not to the swift, nor the
battle to the strong.
(Eccles. 9:11)

Strait is the gate and narrow is the
way that leads unto life.
(Matt. 7:14)

Charity believes and hopes all things.
(1 Cor. 13:7)

The end is not yet.
(Matt. 24:6)

Time and chance happen to all.
(Eccles. 9:11)

DECEPTION
— AND —
APPEARANCE

Beware of false prophets.
(Matt. 7:15)

Meddle not with him that flatters
with his lips.
(Prov. 20:19)

Judge not according to the appearance.
(John 7:24)

Gifts blind the eyes.
(Deut. 16:19)

A little with honesty is better than
a great deal with knavery.
(Ps. 37:16)

There is nothing covered that shall
not be revealed.
(Matt. 10:26; Mark 4:22; Luke 8:17, 12:2)

Profess not knowledge which you
do not have.
(Ecclus. 3:25)

The devil can transform himself into
an angel of light.
(2 Cor. 11:14)

When the blind lead the blind,
both shall fall into the ditch.
(Matt. 15:14; Luke 6:39)

Names and natures do often agree.
(1 Sam. 25:25)

The righteous are bold as a lion.
(Prov. 28:1)

Gold is tried in fire.
(Zech. 13:9; 1 Pet. 1:7)

If you had not plowed with my heifer,
you would not have found out my riddle.
(Judg. 14:18)

A city set on a hill cannot be hid.
(Matt. 5:14)

Let nobody deceive you with
vain words.
(Eph. 5:6)

A good report makes the bones fat.
(Prov. 15:30).

He that digs a pit for another shall
fall into it himself.
(Ps. 7:15; Prov. 26:27; Eccles. 10:8)

Like people, like priest.
(Hos. 4:9)

There is nothing hid that shall
not be known.
(Matt. 10:26; Mark 4:22; Luke 8:17, 12:2)

Birds of a feather flock together.
(Ecclus. 27:9)

Man looks at outside appearance,
but the Lord looks into the heart.
(1 Sam. 16:7)

Beware of a wolf in sheep's clothing.
(Matt. 7:15)

A good name is better than
precious ointment.
(Eccles. 7:1)

Favor is deceitful, and beauty is vain.
(Prov. 31:30)

Don't hide your light under a bushel.
(Matt. 5:15; Mark 4:21; Luke 11:33)

A leopard cannot change his spots.
(Jer. 13:23)

WORK
AND
LAZINESS

As you sow, so you reap.
(Gal. 6:7)

He that will not work shall not eat.
(2 Thess. 3:10)

As the door turns upon its hinges,
so does the slothful upon his bed.
(Prov. 26:14)

The sluggard is wiser in his own
conceit than seven men that can
render a reason.
(Prov. 26:16)

The workman is worthy of his meat.
(Matt. 10:10)

The end of a thing is better
than the beginning.
(Eccles. 7:8)

The sluggard will not plow because
of the cold.
(Prov. 20:4)

Every man must labor in his own trade.
(1 Cor. 7:20)

A worker needs not to be ashamed.
(2 Tim. 2:15)

The sleep of a laboring man is sweet.
(Eccles. 5:12)

The sluggard's guise, loath to go to
bed and loath to rise.
(Prov. 6:9)

He that seeks finds.
(Matt. 7:8)

The sabbath was made for man, and not
man for the sabbath.
(Mark 2:27)

Who sows sparingly shall also
reap sparingly.
(2 Cor. 9:6)

Be content with your wages.
(Luke 3:14)

The slothful man says there is a lion
in the way.
(Prov. 26:13)

He that observes the wind shall
not sow, and he that regards the clouds
shall not reap.
(Eccles. 11:4)

In all labor there is profit.
(Prov. 14:23)

Every man shall bear his own burden.
(Gal. 6:5)

He that tills his land shall be
rewarded with bread.
(Prov. 12:11)

The laborer is worthy of his hire.
(Luke 10:7; 1 Tim. 5:18)

Every man's work shall be
made manifest.
(1 Cor. 3:13)

In the sweat of your brows shall
you eat bread.
(Gen. 3:19)

MEN
AND
WOMEN

Man and wife shall be one flesh.
(Gen. 2:24; Matt. 19:5; Eph. 5:31)

A good wife is a great blessing.
(Ecclus. 26:3)

The husband is the head of the wife.
(Eph. 5:23)

A fair woman without discretion is
like a ring of gold in a swine's snout.
(Prov. 11:22)

Wine and women make wise
men renegades.
(Ecclus. 19:2)

It is better to marry than to burn.
(1 Cor. 7:9)

As the maid, so the mistress.
(Isa. 24:2)

Happy is the husband of a good wife.
(Ecclus. 26:1)

It is not good for a man to be alone.
(Gen. 2:18; Eccles. 4:10)

A virtuous woman is a crown
to her husband.
(Prov. 12:4)

Marriage is honorable.
(Heb. 13:4)

Continuous dropping on a rainy day
and a contentious woman are alike.
(Prov. 27:15)

A woman is the weaker vessel.
(1 Pet. 3:7)

The price of a virtuous woman is far
above rubies.
(Prov. 31:10)

ADVICE
AND
PRUDENCE

You cannot plow with an ox and an
ass together.
(Deut. 22:10)

Nobody puts a piece of new cloth unto
an old garment.
(Matt. 9:16; Mark 3:21)

A little leaven leavens the whole lump.
(1 Cor. 5:6; Gal. 5:9)

Be not overwise in doing your business.
(Ecclus. 10:26)

Thorns make the greatest crackling.
(Eccles. 7:6)

Wolves rend sheep when the
shepherds fail.
(John 10:12)

You cannot make bricks without straw.
(Exod. 5:7)

It is good to bear the yoke
in one's youth.
(Lam. 3:27)

The disciple is not above his master.
(Matt. 10:24; Luke 6:40)

Walk while you have the light.
(John 12:35)

There is safety in numbers.
(Prov. 11:14, 24:6)

The ass doesn't bray when it has
grass, and the ox doesn't low over
his fodder.
(Job 6:5)

Wine is a mocker,
strong drink is raging.
(Prov. 20:1)

A little fire kindles a great matter.
(James 3:5)

Don't muzzle the mouth of the ox that treads out the corn.
(Deut. 25:4; 1 Cor. 9:9; 1 Tim. 5:18)

One cannot gather grapes of thorns or figs of thistles.
(Matt. 7:16)

The dog returns to its vomit.
(Prov. 26:11; 2 Pet. 2:22)

Open not your heart to everybody.
(Ecclus. 8:19)

Little foxes spoil the vines.
(Song of Sol. 2:15)

What you do, do quickly.
(John 13:27)

The dogs eat of the crumbs which fall from their masters' table.
(Matt. 15:27; Mark 7:28)

Two are better than one.
(Eccles. 4:9)

You can't weigh the fire or measure the wind.
(2 Esd. 4:5)

You can't put new wine into
old bottles.
(Matt. 9:17; Mark 2:22; Luke 5:37)

Young ravens must have meat.
(Job 38:41)

Too much honey cloys the stomach.
(Prov. 25:27)

Be patient as Job.
(James 5:11)

It is folly to kick against pricks.
(Acts 9:5)

Be not wise in your own conceits.
(Rom. 12:16)

No man can serve two masters.
(Matt. 6:24; Luke 16:13)

Believe not every tale.
(Ecclus. 19:15)

Do not lean on a broken reed.
(Isa. 36:6)

A living dog is better than a dead lion.
(Eccles. 9:4)

The ox knows his owner,
and the ass his master's crib.
(Isa. 1:3)

The kettle and the earthen pot
don't agree.
(Ecclus. 13:2)

Do not cast pearls before swine.
(Matt. 7:6)

LORD
— AND —
GOD

The Lord gives,
and the Lord takes away.
(Job 1:21)

Obey God rather than men.
(Acts 5:29)

Vengeance belongs only to God.
(Ps. 94:1)

Whom the Lord loves he chastises.
(Prov. 3:12; Heb. 12:6)

All things work together for good to
them that love God.
(Rom. 8:28)

Who puts his trust in the Lord
shall be safe.
(Prov. 29:25)

Man's extremity is God's opportunity.
(Luke 18:27)

God does not forget your work and
labor of love.
(Heb. 6:10)

The word of the Lord endures forever.
(1 Pet. 1:25)

God is a potter and we are the clay.
(Isa. 45:9)

Every perfect gift is from above.
(James 1:17)

The wisdom of this world is
foolishness with God.
(1 Cor. 3:19)

God has power to help and
to cast down.
(2 Chron. 25:8)

What God has joined together, let not
man put asunder.
(Matt. 19:6; Mark 10:9)

Every man has his proper
gift from God.
(1 Cor. 7:7)

The name of the Lord is a tower
of strength.
(Prov. 18:10)

If God be with us,
who can be against us?
(Rom. 8:31)

All things are possible with God.
(Matt. 19:26)

One day is with the Lord as
a thousand years, and a thousand
years as one day.
(2 Pet. 3:8)

God loves a cheerful giver.
(2 Cor. 9:7)

Man proposes, God disposes.
(Prov. 16:9)